# My Day

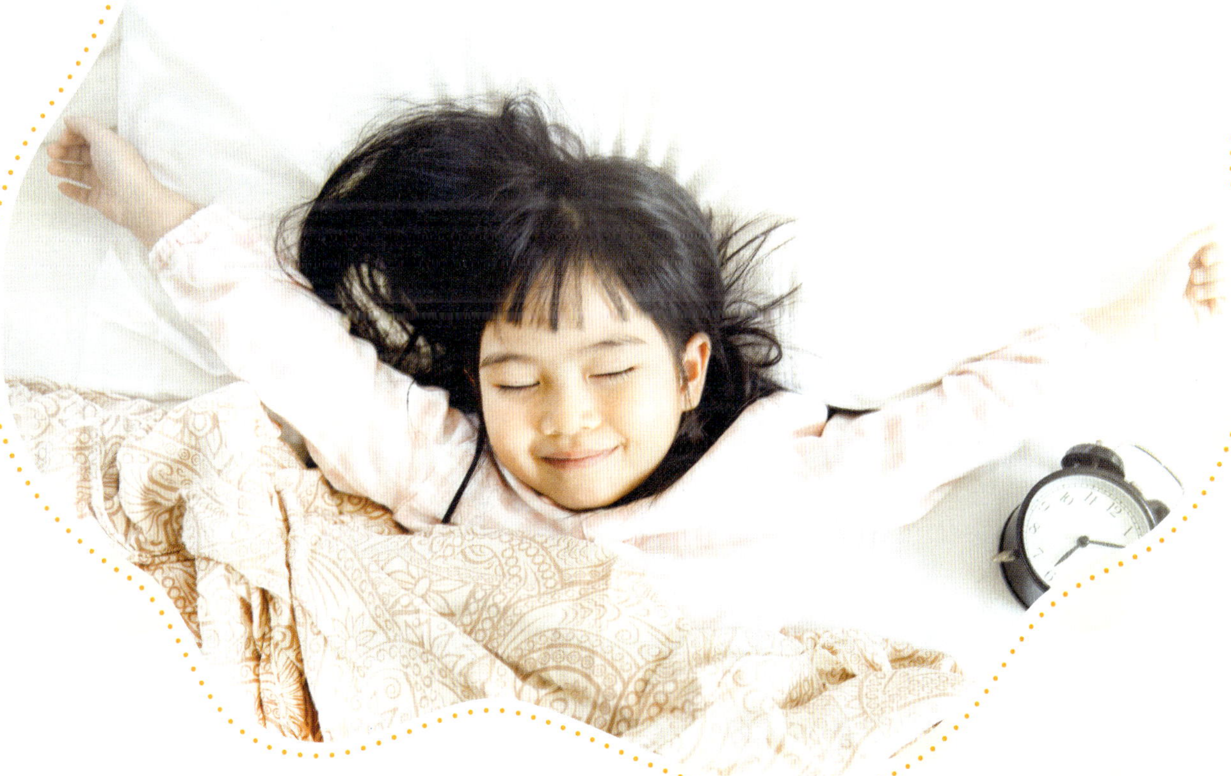

Fabiola Sepulveda

# Notes for the Grown-ups

This wordless book allows for a rich shared reading experience for children who do not yet know how to read words or who are beginning to learn. Children can look at the pages to gather information from what they see, and they can suggest text to tell the story.

# To extend this reading experience, do one or more of the following:

Ask the child to think about the activities shown in the book. Which one is their favorite thing to do?

Ask the child what other pictures might be added to this book to show what else they do each day.

Introduce vocabulary such as these words when looking at the pictures and telling the story you see:

- bath
- brush
- dress
- eat
- I
- me
- play
- read
- school
- sleep
- teeth
- wake

After reading the pictures, come back to the book again and again. Rereading is an excellent tool for building literacy skills.

Encourage the child to narrate the pictures in the story. Say to the child, "Read the story to me. Tell me what the pictures say."

**Consultant**

Cynthia Malo, M.A.Ed.

**Publishing Credits**

Rachelle Cracchiolo, M.S.Ed., *Publisher*
Emily R. Smith, M.A.Ed., *SVP of Content Development*
Véronique Bos, *VP of Creative*
Dona Herweck Rice, *Senior Content Manager*

**Image Credits:** all images from iStock and/or Shutterstock

**Library of Congress Cataloging-in-Publication Data**

Names: Sepulveda, Fabiola, author.
Title: My day / Fabiola Sepulveda.
Description: Huntington Beach, CA : Teacher Created Materials, Inc, 2024. |
  Audience: Ages 3-9. | Summary: This wordless picture book highlights
  activities one might do from sunrise to sunset, allowing the reader to
  narrate their day. Includes notes for the grown-ups.
Identifiers: LCCN 2024003471 (print) | LCCN 2024003472 (ebook) | ISBN
  9798765961094 (paperback) | ISBN 9798765967317 (ebook)
Subjects: CYAC: Stories without words. | Day--Fiction. | LCGFT: Wordless
  picture books.
Classification: LCC PZ7.1.R4548 My 2024  (print) | LCC PZ7.1.R4548  (ebook)
  | DDC [E]--dc23
LC record available at https://lccn.loc.gov/2024003471
LC ebook record available at https://lccn.loc.gov/2024003472

 Teacher
Created
Materials

5482 Argosy Avenue
Huntington Beach, CA 92649
**www.tcmpub.com**
ISBN 979-8-7659-6109-4
© 2024 Teacher Created Materials, Inc.
Printed by 51250
PO 10289 / Printed in USA